Home and Other Foreign Lands

Douglas S. Brown

PRINTED IN THE UNITED STATES OF AMERICA

1st Printing / KDP

Cover Design and Interior Art: Brenda Salomé Salamone

Editor: zenrage

ISBN: 9798543579763

Dedication

This book is dedicated to Frederick E. Tremallo (1933-1998), my writing instructor at Phillips Exeter Academy.

He wrote "yes" or "Yes!" sometimes on a poem or story. He "taught" me that writing was akin to sculpting—what to leave, what to chisel away.

I think he knew he was sculpting me as a writer and person.

I thank him for that.

"This is beyond exceptional. I can't believe I am the only one to comment. Many poets will write a lifetime and not produce a piece as amazing as this one."

–R.L. "The Beautiful Hunger"

"Douglas, you have an unbelievable way with words, the reader hangs on to every word, in suspense…wanting to know more."

–L.G. "A Detective in the House"

"What a lovely poem. Leaves you wanting more. Superbly done, Douglas."

–A.F. "Boundary Waters"

"Douglas, you are so gifted at creating complete scenario and a particular atmosphere. Your talent is amazing. This poem is a FAVE. Awesome."

– L. L. B. "Everything Must Be Filled."

Table of Contents

Chasing The Alligator –1999   1

The Wild Parrots Of Hollywood   3

Los Angeles   5

He Must Have Been Big   9

Mission Exit   15

The Los Angeles River   17

The River   23

The Beautiful Hunger   27

Dancing With Jesus   33

Kansas Hibiscus   39

The Viewing   43

The Bath   47

In City   49

Looking For Bukowski   51

Velvet Elvis   53

No Tree Street Names   57

The Thin Walls Of The Heart   61

I Just Remembered This   65

The Bus Always Comes   67

Chasing The Alligator – 2021   71

Boundary Waters   73

A Detective In The House   75

No Words   79

The Sight Distance Ahead   83

Freja – The Farmers Wife   89

Everything Must Be Filled –Cavalaire-sur-Mer, June 1945   91

Trip To The Black Sea   95

Treblinka's Seven Gardens   97

The Street With No Children   99

The Trip Home   103

Chasing The Alligator

1999

We have lost our sense of wonder.

We chase the alligator

down Front Street,

past Mollies Convenience Store

and the County Clerk-Recorder Office.

He has taken us under

a red sky grand,

hardly noticed.

Were it not for the children

riding on his back,

we would let him go.

They sit on him,

smooth as a new wallet,

shoes, purse.

Where in our imagination,

we ask ourselves,

have we seen this kind of thing before?

Yes, where?

Following the tip of his tail

as he heads for the culvert

we move as one,

an army

uncertain of its purpose.

The Wild Parrots Of Hollywood

He cried

after she held him.

(He had told her

this wasn't his first time.)

The window had been full

of parrots in the palm trees.

They scrawed and heeched

And k-k-ee'd.

She had picked him up back then

and held him

and they both looked out

eyes wide

as he called back to them—

Kee-kee! Haaaw! Schsch!Schsch!

All this he did not say

to her now.

The parrots were gone,

And she was gone.

But she tightened

around him

and he listened.

The sound,

years away and apart,

was the same.

And what she did not tell him—

Green and yellow

flashes

and the many,

straining beating hearts.

Los Angeles

After we met

I thought we really had something,

really hit it off.

It wasn't the words we spoke,

the easy fluorescent trail they made.

Maybe it was the Japanese lantern

glowing over your bare shoulder

or the smile you threw

to the side–

To someone.

Or maybe it was the cool damp air,

slight seduction of rain–

but no rain.

Perfect, cool molecules,

layer on layer,

air sitting on air.

But after, I couldn't find you.

I couldn't find you

in the heavy-sitting valleys,

behind the cool-barriered perfect hedges

with stone guard dogs,

in the palm shadowed boulevards

Or the canyon mazes.

I couldn't find you

in the final exhalations of space,

on sun baked, cracked cement plaza drives.

I couldn't find you

in the starkly lined avenues

amongst the serious-expressioned manikins.

It really is a desert here, huh?

Had said the pale cheeked waiter from Wisconsin

while we waited for you to come back.

Yes, I thought, touching the sweating water-glass.

A stage set in a desert

Filled with mirages and promises

And doors that no one answers

And roads that curve toward the sun.

We both knew you weren't coming back.

I won't find *you* again.

But I will keep looking.

And looking.

And looking.

There is always that chance.

Yes, to find someone like you.

That chance.

I leave alone,

Tip under plate.

A dog barks at my steps,

waits, barks again.

We are both close,

yet impossibly,

far from home.

He Must Have Been Big

Sybil Madison

(her stage name)

and Bernie Dodds

(real name)

weren't nobodies.

She had been in pictures,

he directed

and wrote a few.

You remember–

Those great lines in

Down In The Trenches.

And she–that *look* she gave Cary.

They live high in a palm tree,

in its crown,

just south of Franklin,

on Bronson.

Been there for years.

One day he helped her chase away the wild parrots

and never left.

They hold hands

every sunset

and wander over their memories

looking down at the studios,

mysteriously quiet from above.

Nothing's changed,

she says.

Everything's changed,

he says.

When they plan to go out

she always asks him—

What do I wear?

Wear yourself.

You look beautiful.

I feel beautiful.

And he—

I just want to sit at the Brown Derby,

maybe with Willie.

And she—

I thought Willie was up here,

above McCadden maybe.

Or Normandie, maybe.

I loved the Brown Derby, too.

The new one—

You didn't see it.

And he—

If you'd been Jewish

we could have been together.

Shh dear. Is that the Santa Ana wind coming?

We are together.

Where are you again?

Over near Marilyn, he says,

Village Memorial,

On the ground, not like her,

In one of those damn drawers.

I know, she says,

I was there. Nice service.

And you, he asks her again, like couples do.

I still forget. Golly.

It was all a blur.

Like in a movie.

Kinda.

Or when the film breaks.

You know.

Never mind, he says.

It hardly matters now.

This night the wind is wonderful, warm

and they sway together, car lights fanning streets safely
below.

There! A fire truck—

And somewhere near Fountain—the tiny flickering fire.

They look north.

It is darker and there is only one—

The tallest palm for miles.

It is moving like a wand,

pushed by the Santa Anas.

It is solitary, grand, lonely.

She spots him first.

I think I remember him!

Don't stare, he says.

What was that picture?

The one with the horse,

The horse, the horse.

And the lady, red hair

I think.

Oh, he seems alone.

And he—

He must have been big,

To be up there by Bronson Canyon.

Yeah, she says,

Moving closer to him

In the complete warmth of the high swirling air,

The fronds all around them dancing and bowing.

He must have been big.

Mission Exit

In the far lane

out of the marine fog,

Near Mission Road Exit–

the 5 South–

a 1965 Ford Ranchero,

vein blue

and sea bleached bone white.

The grim-faced driver,

hands at ten and two,

her plum head wrap and

fingers tight as roots,

her face twisted furrows.

I will never know her.

She will hold all she knows–

sacred, broken–

as real as a sharpened knife–

and disappear uncaptured

even by these words.

The Los Angeles River

She drove the 5 North everyday—

Five-thirty, five-forty.

She got to take fifty minutes off

until her second job when

She walked along the Los Angeles River.

No one was nice at either job.

She did things even the men wouldn't do,

cleaning grease from the overhead filters,

cutting out fish guts with a curved knife.

They tried to touch her

but she held out the guts

like it was her own.

She told her Tito and Esmeralda

the wonderful praises she got for her work.

She thought she could leave them

with the ten-thousand dollar insurance policy

she bought from the man at her door.

     It even pays in case of suicide!

He had said cheerfully,

dabbing his sweaty cheeks.

So she paid the fifteen dollars

when he came by each month.

She made her pink-haired neighbor the beneficiary

and gave her subtle hints—

     You never know when you will become

     a parent!

She made sure to spell the name right

and put the right address.

Carlye Dombrynski.

She did not want her children

to see her disintegrate

in shame.

She decided to end it

in Egret Park under the 5.

She bought the pills at La Pharmacia

and the man crossed himself.

> *My last day on this Earth.*

> *I hope I am accepted in the trading of my life*

> *to help them.*

She drove over the overpass and looked

down at the Home Depot and the train yard.

And then she saw a green-yellow parrot flying under
the 5.

She could feel the color

move under her, unperturbed

and beautiful and still,

a perfect vibration of balance and passion

like the few times she had really made love

to their father,

before he had left them.

She thought it must be

a sign from an ancient people

who lived here before

and struggled like she did.

The day she had visited the Park

A *pasajero* had told her—

> The ancients lived here,
>
> Fished and hunted right here!
>
> They made their life.
>
> Women cleaned, cooked, men caught fish and game,
>
> They made love right over there—

He pointed and her eyes followed:

> That is where I will die then.

The dirty wise man must have been an oraculo,

or a professor,

to see the past like a dream.

But he did not recognize her.

I am like all the women before.

A flash of beauty on a river,

worn out hands from pounding and cleaning,

barely able to touch a man with smoothness,

to live and then disappear and live again.

She drove on to Los Feliz Boulevard and got off

and walked along the River

throwing the pills down the bank.

　　Excuse me for living!

She said to the people

who break hearts

　　And breaking my commitment

　　to you.

　　But I am here,

　　I am still here.

　　Living and continuing

　　Free, like the ever-walking

　　Spirits from the river's bend.

　　And the green parrot

　　Who also escaped its cage.

I think I know this.

I know this!

She ran back

and got in the bath with her kids

rubbing them with the special soap from home until they squealed.

You are not working today, mother?

No, I am with you today.

I am with you.

The River

I have put the River away,

not far

near the slabs of cold memory

and the ashes of the Chumash.

The sun may warm it,

yes, turning as it may

the reflections of lives lived

like gentle stones

casting back

from its currents.

Into that River

goes the noble, hobbled tree.

Goes my child, only one,

my heart,

arms like bare roots

searching for the shore.

She goes this way.

The peace I get from your touch

goes,

the sunset,

the desert dawn.

The opera my aunt played

bringing sweaty, stinging, summer tears

onto her pink porch.

All goes.

A moment when nothing is said

between lovers–

All goes

to the River.

The face remembered just before sleep.

Barely noticed windows

of neighbors' dusk lives,

like the *flick, flick*

of a slide projector

on the wall.

All.

The glance of light

off your hip

when you wait for me.

Even you ask—Why must?—

And seeing your words land,

Softer than sand

and disappear under

you leave them as buoys

to drift next to mine,

or someone's.

The Beautiful Hunger

She could see pink

over the vanity that her husband had built.

Someone had removed the mirror,

oh, long ago

and put it in the alcove with the window

so she could sit and look over the cemetery and

into the mountains.

She could see the pink

and the vault of warmth over

the mountains,

and some purple glowing on the rises;

even through cataracts.

But not the lights of the helicopter

flying over Alhambra.

She used to take a daily walk

to Obregon Park

and even to Belvedere School to watch

her granddaughter play.

But now her granddaughter watched her

and carefully laid her in bed

after she fell asleep in the alcove.

Tonight she felt the hand on her shoulder

and saw her nieta place food

on the small table next to her.

> *I can smell snow on the peaks.*
> *I am not hungry.*
> *I want to be eaten.*

Nieta drew back.

You mean eaten by God?

She only smiled and turned back to the window.

The wolf looked out at the valley

and saw an enormous bathing of pink and orange light

which caused cubs nearby to sniff the air

 and pause before rolling in the snow,

fighting.

She sniffed for his smell

but it was not there.

She sniffed for the Early People

whose bones she had found.

Nothing.

A cub rushed her and she snarled weakly.

Where is the mother?

Then some meat was dropped

at the cave's entrance.

She sniffed it and settled more deeply

into the cave's bedding.
She looked down at the moving ribbons

of white and red which always blossomed at night.

I want to be eaten.

By the Early People

with their clean killing

not shot at from strange mechanical birds.

I am ready to be eaten.

She looked out across the ribbons

and the pink and sniffed the air.

There is someone.

There is someone.

A wolf in a woman's heart.

Nieta found her with her eyes

and her mouth wide open

staring down this time.

She paused before she lifted her up
and looked out into

the faded pink sky,

the purple rises and the faded strokes of sun.

And then she thought–

What a good day to be eaten.

A woman in a wolf's heart!

Must be the stories

that my grandmother told me of the Early People.

This time she was not embarrassed
to have these thoughts.

She put her gently in bed and covered her

and hurried down to her own daughter's bed

and got under the covers.

She held her tightly until she could

feel the gentle thump – thump – thump

and protect her from the inevitable, beautiful

hunger.

Dancing With Jesus

Van Nuys.

She hated the words.

They meant nothing.

She cried the first day and was left alone.

Except for prayer time.

It seemed like the bells were always ringing.

The room was small, yet longer than

her bedroom in El Paso.

She put her hand out the window

but Ranger didn't lick it or breathe

into her cupped hand.

She was on the second floor.

Someone had a left a white flower in a vase on her
dresser.

The Mistress brought her dinner

and nodded quietly

when she said she wanted to go home.

To her Alfredo, who had been on his way to propose.

That is the only thing I would let you go for,

he had said.

They had danced the Saturday before

and she could feel his arm around her.

Was that love?

She fell asleep in the unfamiliar,

stiff bed, sheets starched taut,

the stirring of winds pushed from far away

breathing in on her like a giant ghost.

In her dream a man came up to her

after work while she sat on the dock,

her last day there.

She jumped down to walk away

but he smiled and held up his hand for her.

She blushed and walked to him.

She swirled and there he was.

His boots were like

a mirror,

his eyes like a lake.

They danced and danced until

she heard her father's voice,

looked away and he was gone.

She woke to someone gently shaking her.

It was still dark.

She thought she smelled smoke.

She heard sirens in the distance.

It is the Santa Anas.

We must serve,

said the Aspirant.

She dressed quickly

and ran down to Prayers

which were hurried.

Young women got on a bus

and were passed out warm rolls to eat.

She still felt him and smiled.

The Mistress stood and said—

This is what we do.

The Valley is on fire

and we will care for the people.

We serve.

Mistress Clara looked right at her.

Did she know about my dream?

Should I have dreamt about

dancing with Our Lord?

She blushed again and looked out

at smoke and ash

and the desperate, scurrying people.

She fed the people

who were tired and beaten.

The fires were still in their eyes.

She smiled at them and they smiled.

Sisters worked serving the food

and passing blankets and arranging cots.

Someday I will dress like them.

Not like this, like a girl.

Carrying diapers to a young mother

she thought of the dance.

Elvis? A Waltz?

It seemed like both.

She hummed the music.

She saw his face.

It was—a face.

She saw what he saw.

A great wind-swept desert.

The young mother smiled,

The baby cried.

The fires flickered in the window panes.

She held the baby.

The mother closed her tearing eyes.

She knew her place.

It was right here,

here beneath the Great Basin

in the canyons of greatest need.

Kansas Hibiscus

She watched her move

the potted Chinese Hibiscus inside,

sliding it over the not yet frozen ground,

hefting it slowly over the six wood back steps,

resting and breathing,

hands on hips.

Each year she would think of helping.

But she didn't

and this time she could tell,

she was really struggling.

No one was there to help her.

A few years ago she had told her–

  "Scarlet Rose Mallow.

  Only plant it. Cut it back late fall

  and leave it in the ground."

But her friend had not listened.

She hadn't listened to other things.

But they were neighbors

and she was from the somewhere,

Los Angeles,

somewhere,

and they don't listen,

everybody knew.

Her neighbor had been surprised

when she had buried her husband

in the back

with a simple stone

next to a row of them.

She could see them bloom,

five pedals for each of their children,

and sit with him anytime, any weather.

Her western neighbor

had to go all the way to the

Church cemetery

and shiver or hide under a parka.,

to visit hers.

So today,

after the struggle was over,

she made some tea

and walked the distance,

cups and saucers on a tray,

imperfectly matched and unbalanced.

It was about time

they put differences aside.

The Viewing

She wore it that weekend

after he bought it at the drugstore

with eight dollars

they didn't have.

Rent money.

Food.

It was a man's Timex

and she wore it

in the motel.

She wore it in the waves

at the beach in Coronado.

The hands froze

and sand collected.

She wore it to the wedding.

She wore it on their honeymoon.

A night on Catalina.

Eleven-thirty eight.

She said that was when they

fell in love.

She wore it to the hospital

until the doctor talked about

stillborn and heart beats.

Then it was gone.

And she.

Now, forty-five years later

he waited until everybody

walked past her.

Nobody knew

husband number one

from long ago.

A grandchild smiled at him.

Some lawyer had found him.

Finally, he got up.

He couldn't look at her face

but saw her wrist

with the Timex watch.

The wrist underneath

that he used to kiss

leading to other things

and a baby

with no breath, blue.

He saw the hour's hand

floating on the sand

on the dial.

Minutes still thirty-eight.

He saw her hair floating

in the wind

and the sea rushing to engulf her

and take her

for the moment.

and reappear

like now

laughing,

love really not lost

at all.

The Bath

My mother arrives

letting in briefly

the dim, smokey sun.

Her fingers are red-raw.

Without listening

I know my job

and I get the worn pliers,

landlord-loaned

to turn on the bath.

My brother stands

jittery and exposed

while the water runs too hot

over his feet.

He sits without warning,

used to the pain.

He is clean.

I put a towel around him.

After the water has drained

We listen carefully,

my brother's face

gleefully bright.

There it is!

There is the clucking rasp

Of mother's snore,

measured yet unpredictable sounds.

We cling to them

in muted joy.

In City

I still walk your streets

for the untended curb,

the flattened can,

the half-opened shade.

I am in the dark,

un-spilled light,

uninspected.

I am caught

in the city of cautious regard.

I am not violent

but I wonder what it would take

to crack the cement

and bend the rebar

to let a man out.

Looking For Bukowski

I finally gave up

and then found him

in East LA,

Carlton Way.

Covered in vomit.

Bottle of Tanqueray

propping up his head.

I knelt down

earnestly

waiting.

Fuck you,

he finally said.

A real word.

Real words.

Two.

Fucking perfect.

Velvet Elvis

There were two things—

The sound of my parents,

laughing and dancing, wrestling,

the wall by my bed a tight drum to their early love.

And there was the second thing—

The velvet man in the hallway,

His eyes following me to and from the bathroom,

Appraising me all the way.

Let's see what you can do, rabbit slipper feet man!

And my Mom smiled at him everyday

and Dad saluted.

The King!

And so he was, in that two-bedroom second story,

above the tire man

and the dry-waller.

Dark nights of wrenching, sweat-soaked dreams,

gigantic black pressing shapes,

were soothed by him

and my Mom singing

Uh-uh, uh-uh, Darlin'.

Night terrors,

She'd say under her breath—

Last life's death haunting you.

Mom's folk were Navajo,

so she told me,

to explain it all,

cooling my forehead with a facecloth.

The velvet man told me—

Be brave at school,

Fight and stand up for yourself,

Be a man but treat the ladies nice.

So, I did.

His gaze became proud.

After he left,

The home was just me and Mom.

We'd look at where he used to be,

A square of missing space,

Outlined faintly with no explanation.

Mom and I would take a bath together

but she would stay under too long,

her hair floating up like boiling, hopeless noodles.

her skin would be as red as her eyes.

The tire man would visit

and bring us container dinner.

He'd stare, hard, when she and I danced together

And he'd drink beer until my bed-time.

There was no laughter into my drum.

Just a relentless struggle to fill the empty spaces.

The velvet man was gone.

I visited my Dad.

I was fourteen,

and he was nearly dead from living.

I brought him a new Velvet Man

from Juniors All Purpose Market.

I broke her heart and yours.

Keep it, he said.

So, he is on the mantel now.

My own two girls

think he is a sequin Jesus without a beard.

Close, but not quite.

A man,

maybe a real man

opening the hearts

of the truly, profoundly innocent

and leaving redemption

a touch out of grasp.

It is why we four dance until we drop.

No Tree Street Names

He built motels

across America

loving the land so much

he could sleep anywhere

on her

in her

cheaply,

predictably.

Anywhere was home to him.

Home was not special

but same.

Same bars of soap,

same color wrappers.

Same towels.

Same smells almost.

Same views.

Home across

the human spirit

of imaginary states.

Just outside streets

with tree names.

And out of this

I arrived

from love created for each single

completed

square space

spilling forward,

motel to motel,

born by American Motel Woman,

timeless builder,

faceless

with no Kodachrome

to pin down my origin

or capture their sulfur-tipped passion.

Pick-up truck front seat cradles,

beer for sedative,

K-Mart toys,

all-night pharmacies.

His gift—

I belong anywhere,

nowhere,

owe nothing,

know anyone,

no one,

am rooted in spackle,

drywall

and cheap two-by-fours

and need only decide

which illusions

to put up

and which to take down.

The Thin Walls Of The Heart

Finally,

came the sounds

of orgasms

much like the sounds from a stage

as though you were the director

in the back, dark,

straining to get it,

if it sounded real enough.

It was the first joyful

pain straining sound in days

distanced from the bitter Fuck Yous,

the tearful phone slams

and Leave-Me-Alones.

I followed their story

like the Late Night News,

wondering when—if—I should call the police.

I judged: when the man's voice raised above the woman's.

It never happened.

The door slams were hers—you could tell.

Women pitch a ball the same way.

Still, it comes back at you hard

in other ways.

So, startled I woke up—

How long would it take them?

Was it deep or meaningless or selfish or showy?

Why weren't there bed noises like when

they had fought?

Is it a new lover?

Are they on the couch?

And then, echoing throughout the Spanish style

apartment complex

others, I supposed,

like me

sensed the conclusion–

Or are they, too, disappointed?

There is no grammar in love

so that explains its emptiness.

And the so what? of it.

It was short, by the clock.

Then, nothing.

Not even a murmur.

The next day I walked underneath, curious.

What does it take to prove love?

Or caution murder?

The two are like strings from

the same piece of dynamite.

I drive to work,

hoping not to die.

I Just Remembered This

I just remembered this—

The Santa Anas were blowing hard.

I woke up and stood at the patio door.

The table outside,

its round glass top, lifted perfectly,

magically up, floated, and then down and shattered.

The physics and the timing were perfect.

Some ancient stirring told me to look for an answer,

perhaps a revelation.

But I went back to bed

 and just now, years later got it—

   The glass rose and fell.

The Bus Always Comes

The guy was sideways

on the bus bench,

Hollywood and Edgemont.

Nothing except yellow-tape

in a square around him.

A woman waited for her bus,

bags at her side

a respectable distance away.

She was looking down the boulevard,

past him

for her bus.

Chasing The Alligator

2021

We have lost our sense of history.

We chase the alligator

down Front Street,

past Mollies Convenience Store

and the County Clerk-Recorder Office.

He's taken us under

a red sky grand,

hardly noticed.

Were it not for the children

riding on his back,

we would let him go.

They sit on him,

smooth as a new wallet,

shoes, purse.

Where in our imagination,

we ask ourselves,

have we seen this kind of thing before?

Yes, where?

Following the tip of his tail

as he heads for the culvert

we move as one,

      an army

      uncertain of its purpose.

Boundary Waters

The man rested his paddle carefully

next to the bundle.

    My favorite time of day.

    Dusk.

The light was soft,

The water still as lakeside glass,

insects skimming over touching,

laying down a perfect parabola

and then touching again.

He still felt her kiss and touch

on cheek and hand.

He smiled at the bundle.

Everything I need and more.

Sometime back a ways,

paddling easy in a light chop,

he had forgotten to worry about it.

    What did doctors know.

Resting, he had taken a cookie

from the bundle and ate it,

looking at each bite before.

Dusk left him and the canoe went on,

    paddle easy,

    paddle strong, paddle easy, paddle strong.

Surely, he had crossed it by now.

And surely who gives a—

His sudden laughter startled a Great Blue Heron.

It flew up, its wings a miracle.

The man let the canoe drift

and looked to the beautiful darkening sky.

He took another cookie from the bundle.

    I am ready.

    I am ready.

A Detective In The House

The clues are there.

The notes.

The writing.

The phone numbers.

The calendar.

Especially the calendar

holding all the secrets

of what was done and will be done.

He is bent over the cubby-holed desk,

slippers, flannel bathrobe,

searching through the familiar

and seeing only the hidden,

the missing,

the opaque.

The crime?

Something stolen, precious

and worse,

it is just out of sight,

next to the words,

the notes, the writing,

the calendar.

Especially the calendar.

So obvious the number,

the day,

yet not now the season.

He finds her worried face again

and continues.

All those around him

keep it from him—

the secret is—

nothing is gone,

nothing was done.

The detective searches

for himself in the clues

of unravelling time.

No Words

She was with me up until—

What was it?

The 37th or 44th visit.

A smile.

A word. Or two.

Time to pee.

Fluorescent lights

Smiling laughing nurses.

Good-hearted.

A few dim with their own thoughts.

But carefully not carrying anyone else's.

The best built machines were in rooms by themselves.

Quiet.

Attendants smoked outside

and dark-faced figures carrying

lifeless flowers hurried by,

practiced words trailing behind them.

I am in the wrong wing.

A woman escapes her straps,

her red hair and speech wild.

Her body no use anymore

but to get out of.

She is gently tied to a chair and talks to

me as I go by—explaining her plans.

This floor smells of the Wait.

Other wives, grandmothers, mothers talk

in front of sadly hanging televisions each

with many important words.

Their diapers are a final ridicule for

a lifetime of great, earned knowledge.

Where are the men?

I am walking down hallway after hallway.

Color coded floors lead me past you

I am sure and past you once more.

I need to ask at the desks again

and again, I am lost.

You have been moved

and you can't tell me.

There were many words I had needed

to know.

Important terms.

Stage four.

Metastasis.

Early on—alopecia.

What do I do with them now?

I find the room. You.

I am lost in the

untethered, frayed end of explanation.

And terms.

And you are unmoored,

waiting. Patient.

Drifting.

At the end we both, finally,

share no words.

Like in our beginning

when no words

was love.

The Slight Distance Ahead

He lost her that night.

Before—

Weeks after school and weekends,

weather or not,

they had built the fort—

strong, Indian proof.

Father had provided a tarp.

and his father's High Standard Sport 22 pistol

for wild animals.

The woods behind the fort

were near the old highway

used by hunters, vagrants occasionally.

Mostly deer.

Mother could see the fort's flag,

which she had sewn,

from her kitchen window.

Part pirate, part cowboy.

His sister was good at tying boughs together for the walls.

He gathered flat stones from the dried riverbed

for the floor.

Test night he brought a sleeping bag

and signaled to Mother with the lamp

before he tried to sleep.

Sounds kept him awake.

He clutched the 22

until it got hot.

But next morning he went in to breakfast

and ate eagerly.

He had made the distance.

His sister stared at him

across the table,

stirring her cereal.

Jealous.

The night she came out

shivering, to join him,

she brought peanut butter and bread–

No knife.

He walked back to get her a blanket

and the knife for the sandwiches,

22 flapping in the revolver holster.

Mother and Father were in the living room

Drinks with friends.

They saw him

Smiled, turned again to their guests.

He walked back.

She was not there.

He called and walked until scratched, bruised.

Tired, he fell back into the fort.

She must be back in her bed.

After, Mother spent nights sleeping in the fort

until he and Father moved away from her.

No bones were found when

the woods were parceled,

developed.

He would go back and drive the new streets,

looking for her.

He would look for her

in places where he was.

What are you thinking about?

They would often ask him.

But he could not tell them.

He carried the slight distance beyond which

she had gone,

often reached into it for her.

And found it went and went,

stretching, stretched

away,

like anyone's life,

except his own.

Freja – The Farmers Wife

Day's knife is in night's sheath

The moon's eye is covered.

She sits over their scattered bones

feeling only the cold dirt

and the swirling fog.

Her hand grips for the hilt

and she hears the singing blade.

The flails are only for threshing now,

passions are muted.

Those that swarmed with her

on these hills

wait for her command,

her voice to sing out over the field

and raise them up.

It is worth dying here again for you.

Each next day

she puts down her basket,

kneels down to fill it, full.

"Things grow well under

your hands" he says, proudly.

She stands alone now,

the day done,

hands on hips,

baby in the grass

feeling the blood surge

and hearts flame.

They are ready to storm with her over the potatoes

turnips, onions

laughter and moans filling the air

with the sound of sweet, sweet

battle.

Everything Must Be Filled

Cavalaire-sur-Mer, June 1945

We lay on the rough sandy oval rug,

A sign outside our window with an electric arrow

pointed through the window perfectly

to your navel

which I kissed

down to the hair line.

You smelled of seaweed and sand.

I rested my chin on

the soft spot above bone

And remembered

how peaceful

a resting place this was.

As I pleased you

I saw a shadow stop under the door—

It is okay to listen.

Anyone can listen now.

We had not yet shared names.

After, we went below to the café.

We smoked the unapologetic cigarettes of your
country,

pouring out our words

like two waterfalls,

filling the same void.

We sat on precarious, worn stools,

on chapped skin

until the late afternoon sea breeze

pushed us in.

At dusk

we lay on the coiled, tired mattress springs,

hips and toes touching.

We fell asleep

and shared dreams

and went back and forth

into the other's body.

We awoke,

jolted back,

startled to have lost

who we were in the other.

We shared our names then

and pulled up the starchy sheet

and blanket worn thin

from so many strangers.

I am sure you repeated my name.

as I did yours.

The noises came in

and filled us—

    horns, laughter, a yell,

    clinking of coins, glasses and heavy porcelain
plates meeting

    and the sound

    of restless, searching air.

We listened and listened

to catch

where the world's heart had stopped

and when it had started,

again.

Trip To The Black Sea

How to write about such a thing?

Stalin in his vacation train across Ukraine to Sochi—

Eating and drinking, full, talkative.

A smoke or two. A nap.

And the children in the barracks

wanting only to die outside in the air,

brother clutching sister,

sister sister.

Bread,

and then nothing.

Oysters, salmon, pork loin,

steamed vegetables—wine.

He ate what they could not imagine in a dream.

They dreamed of dying with the clouds.

He of wheat harvested by skeletons.

Treblinka's Seven Gardens

She was neither dead

nor alive.

Her feet crunched the ash.

> *Nothing will ever grow here.*

Others came out with her,

lightly stepping,

then stamping.

> *Nothing can grow here.*

Seven spaces,

irregular geometries of in between,

neither light nor dark,

grieving or gay,

forgiven or

revenged.

She was what *they* had feared—

A true Angel of Death,

to keep the boundaries

preserved,

the life chased away.

To remind—

    See,

    see here,

    what nothing really is.

The Street With No Children

No children,

someone decided,

would solve many of today's problems.

So, the street with no children

was experimentally started.

Those that went on it

could observe how quiet it was

and still,

none of the nasty tangles that come with new life

were present.

The stress of the future was lifted

in this sector.

All was silent, unmoving and unthreatening.

And so, someone said—

Peace is here.

And someone else said—

Death begins here.

The trees themselves are giving up

and there is no point to the playing of cats

and the sounds that the wind makes

are gone

and the mothers-to-be stare out of kitchen windows

with nothing to do.

More life is needed than can possibly be handled

by anyone

even to put God in his place

and elders closer to their graves

and sleepless nights

and hopeless fights.

I walk that street now

glad of the screams and shouts,

laughter and crying

and glad that we learned–

    Didn't we?

from Germany,

Russia, China–

to build the streets for children.

The Trip Home

She got out at the dimly lit bus station–"Soderborough", the sign said. The bus driver, over the intercom, said, "Sodburg".

She wanted to stretch her legs, buy a machine coffee-get out, away from the falsely fresh bus air.

A few others-there weren't many on the bus-came after her like released prisoners, wearing night's hood, apprehensively looking around, checking now and again that the driver hadn't quietly slid the bus into the gloom of the late Kansas fall, abandoning them to an uncertain freedom.

She also wanted to wash again. She was sure that the other passengers, even the driver and the ticket man, could smell her. She went in to the bathroom and stood at the sink and looked at her face. Dark purple circles under eyes made her look somehow exotic, she thought, but the tired, deeply wrinkled skin gave away no glamour, only use beyond worn use, like a hand farm tool worn down to perfection. Her hair was wiry and gray, uncontrollable so cut severely short.

She got the water hot and washed her hands and arms and tried to scrub her nails. She inhaled the bile smell, the rot, the fecal smell, the dried blood, the repulsive air that anyone around her could not possibly avoid. It seemed to surround her and grow even as she wished it down the drain.

A woman entered behind her, startling her, and she knocked the paper coffee cup off the sink.

"I'm sorry," the woman said, moving hurriedly into a stall.

"It's okay," she said to the sink. "Not your fault." It was strange to hear her own hollow voice.

The hot water felt good. The slightly scented soap somewhat deflected the years and years of decay. She remembered when she had taken the mattress out herself. She had hauled it to a field and poured gasoline on it and burned it. She had watched it burn until it was only a glowing heap. And then days later she had come back out and stomped the ashes and remains into the ground.

She moisturized her lips with a balm she had bought the night before at the station store. What an extravagance, she had thought. Her lips had lost any suppleness, any fullness-only dry, cracked lines, straight, hard, unyielding, any humor or ease drawn out of them after months of being at her side.

She tried to smile. A bloody crack appeared. She dabbed her mouth with tissue. She heard the flush and rolled her sleeves forward.

The woman came to the sink next to her. She was small, smooth skinned, fresh, with her long shiny black hair tied back neatly in a swirling bun.

"Long night," she said.

"Yes."

"Going home?"

"Yes."

"I am going to take care of my mother."

"Oh." The smaller woman looked down. She put her hands to her face.

"Ill?"

"Well, if you call dying..."

"Oh, I see."

"No one else..." she trailed off, leaving the water running in her sink, lost, staring at it swirling. "No one else..."

"Would help?"

"Yes! That is it. She is way out there in the country. My brothers, even my sister...She refuses to 'go to town' she calls it, for help. She won't leave the family homestead."

"Hum." The smaller woman looked up at her and waited then gathered up her bag and they both left the bathroom. They walked together and each got a machine coffee and machine Danish.

They walked to the bus.

She let the smaller woman go ahead and thought about sitting with her but found her own seat and settled in. She put her coffee and the Danish on the arm rest. She put the pillow, the only thing she had salvaged, on her lap. The smell of death came back. It was in her pocketbook and the carry-on bag and her folded sweater. It was coming out with the steam from the coffee.

The bus backed out and then pulled away. The interior lights dimmed. She watched as several intersections passed and the town receded.

She thought of her husband's last words, years ago.

"You go then. She will suck you in and never let you out. Don't count on me waiting. This is your home—you can have it—she gave it to you. That is that. But I gotta live."

She felt where the wedding band had been. The skin was rough, the joint above ached.

She finished the coffee and then checked her bag for the key to her house-the kitchen door. No one in the town ever went through a front door unless there was a death. But even then, during war times the Western Union men were polite enough to stand outside the kitchen door and wait. Her mother had told her that. There was a way to be tasteful about death.

She felt the key. It was a new one her husband had sent two years ago. He hadn't come to the funeral. No one had. She had sat alone waiting for tears. None came either. She had felt bitter and absolute emptiness. Maybe a tinge of guilt-and then nothing. Two and a half years of bedside, bathroom sitting attendance with a rare wheelchair trip outside as far as the end of the driveway until she had gotten too cold even in the summer and waved her hand, purple and gnarled to go back in. Bathing her, cleaning her foul stained body, turning her in her stained bed, putting food in a toothless, scowling mouth.

Even the slew of words aimed at her, the sundown barrage, she thought of it-even it was a relief from the touching of the body.

"You are the worst daughter anyone ever had."

"You kept your brother from coming to take care of me."

"You stole my notebook with his address and phone number."

"You are keeping me here to steal all my money."

"I am your prisoner and you are trying to kill me."

She would offer her mother the phone to call the police- "You paid them off!"

And then, in the morning, sweetness.

"You need to go back to your life. I will be okay here. I can take care of myself now. Just show me how to work the remote again."

And then the end. She had heard about the last sign of alertness shortly before death. Her mother had wanted to see her garden. There was nothing in it, just dirt clods and a broken fence, but she had wheeled her out and her mother had told her in detail about what vegetables she had planted, who had liked what vegetable, and had described the colors, the years and size of her best yields.

"You liked turnips and no one else did so I grew them over there."

The next day her breathing had become very slowed and then became a rattling sound. She had turned blue. She had sat there and held her mother's hand until it stopped and then for some time after that feeling nothing. She had looked at her mother's face, waiting. Would she suddenly come back?

She had called the nurse and the mortuary and went outside and walked into the fallow field that belonged to the neighbor who was nearly as old as her mother. She had looked at the sun barely showing through dark clouds. She had knelt down and felt the dirt, crumbling a piece in her hand. She remembered picking out a piece of dirt from this same field during a battle with her brothers. It had felt hard. She had thrown it and her brother fell to the ground holding his right eye.

"That was against the rules-no rocks!" He had lost the eye. She had had no friends that year. Only Dusty their dog who forgot to get out of the way when the oil man came to fill their tank.

The van had arrived to take her mother. She was sure now. It was over. A body is a distinctly empty thing after death. It seemed odd to afford it so much dignity. Or any dignity. Dust to dust. Didn't people believe that?

She had had stayed on, sold the house quickly after cleaning it for three days. She had closed her mother's bank account. A young couple had bought it but had avoided inspecting the bedroom.

After the funeral, she packed one bag, called the taxi man and went to the bus station. Besides shopping at Merritts she hadn't been out this far for two and a half years. Had she exhaled in those years? No, everything, she thought, everything, everything was in her.

Just as she nodded off, she felt a gentle touch on her shoulder and she jerked.

"I seem to be making a habit of startling you. And apologizing."

She made a patting motion for the smooth skinned woman to sit next to her. They sat quietly for some minutes and she felt her eyes start to close again.

"You don't mind me asking…but I kind of thought you might have some advice…"

"I was with her for two and a half years. Sole caregiver. I think the Lord had even backed off."

"Was it…?"

"It simply was."

"How did you…?"

"There was no choice."

"That is how I feel, really, except I want to run away and you obviously didn't."

"Of course."

"But I am not…"

"No." A few minutes went by. She could see nothing outside the windows. There were no lights. Other than the droning of the tires and the whine of the engine they might not have been moving anywhere.

"You know what I am really afraid of, like in those magazines, is putting a pillow over her and..." She started to laugh and then covered her mouth and then it came out uncontrollably for some minutes, big rolling tears falling over the smooth skin onto her breast.

"Did you ever have those thoughts?" she managed finally, dabbing her face with a bright pink handkerchief.

"How do you know I didn't?" She lifted up her pillow carefully and showed it to the woman then firmly pressed it down on her lap, hard. She looked over at the woman and felt the first smile, the first exhalation, the first words really that she had had since it had started.

"Oh my!" The smooth skinned woman's eyes flashed and she regarded her intently. "Oh my! What do we have to do? What do we have to do?"

She took the small woman's hands in hers, feeling the smooth, tight skin, feeling the pulse, steady, under. And then something like death—or life—flowed one to the other, uninterrupted, unchallenged, as cleansing as the sudden storm that swept down on them and the bus.

I have been writing poetry and short stories for fifty-five years. I have been published in various poetry magazines and two poetry collections.

My father and mother were my biggest fans. I self-published my first book of poetry in 2014. My mother and father would read the poems to each other. My father passed in 2014.

I have been encouraged over the last few years by readers who told me I should be published.

I have been supported immensely by my wife, Gail Colby.

Hence, "Home and Other Foreign Lands."

My wish is that some of these poems will stand there, by themselves, for you, the reader.

They are for you, after all.

Douglas Brown

Made in the USA
Las Vegas, NV
02 September 2021

29499124R00069